OBLIVIO GATE

Crab Orchard Series in Poetry

First Book Award

OBLIVIO GATE

Sean Nevin

Crab Orchard Review

&

Southern Illinois University Press

Carbondale

11   10   09   08   4   3   2   1

The Crab Orchard Series in Poetry is a joint publishing venture of Southern Illinois
University Press and *Crab Orchard Review.* This series has been made possible by the
generous support of the Office of the President of Southern Illinois University and the
Office of the Vice Chancellor for Academic Affairs and Provost at Southern Illinois
University Carbondale.

Crab Orchard Series in Poetry Editor: Jon Tribble

First Book Award Judge for 2007: Lynne McMahon

Library of Congress Cataloging-in-Publication Data
Nevin, Sean, date.
    Oblivio gate / Sean Nevin.
        p. cm. — (Crab Orchard series in poetry)
    ISBN-13: 978-0-8093-2877-2 (alk. paper)
    ISBN-10: 0-8093-2877-1 (alk. paper)
    I. Title.
    PS3614.E556O25   2008
    811'6—dc22   2008007835

Printed on recycled paper. ♻

The paper used in this publication meets the minimum requirements of American
National Standard for Information Sciences—Permanence of Paper for Printed
Library Materials, ANSI Z39.48-1992. ∞

For my family, for all the families

And for Amelia

Last scene of all,

that ends this strange eventful history,

is second childishness and mere oblivion,

sans teeth, sans eyes, sans taste, sans

everything.

—*William Shakespeare*

Contents

Acknowledgments

Grateful acknowledgment is made to the editors of the following publications, in which these poems previously appeared, some in slightly different form:

The Alsop Review—"September, North Fullerton Avenue" (under the title "Memory")
Blackbird: An Online Journal of Literature and the Arts—"Alzheimer's"
Cutthroat: A Journal of the Arts—"Fainting at My Grandfather's Funeral"
DMQ Review—"The Incident"
42 Opus—"Wildfire Triptych, "Hinged Double Sonnet for the Luna Moths," "Wisdom," and "Elegy"
42 Opus—"Wildfire Triptych"
The Gettysburg Review—"Solomon's Palimpsest"
Journal of the American Medical Association—"Losing Solomon"
The Ledge—"Walking Bees"
North American Review—"Hippocampus" and "The Carpenter Bee"
LOCUSPOINT—"Montclair Vespers," "Solomon's Tool Shed," "Working and Singing," "Heart of the Tyrant King," and "The Other Dream in Which He Is Weightless"
RUNES: A Review of Poetry—"Oblivio Gate"
Pistola—"Self-Portraits from the Widow House," "Self-Portrait as Tithonus," and "Self-Portrait as Aurora"

"Losing Solomon" was featured on Verse Daily and also appeared in the anthology *Family Matters: Poems of our Families* (Bottom Dog Press, 2006).

"Hinged Double Sonnet for the Luna Moths" was chosen for inclusion in the Poetry Everywhere project, a series of short films featuring animated interpretations of contemporary poetry, created by the Poetry Foundation in collaboration with the Creative Writing and Film Department of the University of Wisconsin–Milwaukee.

"Again, the Gnome and I Catch Dawn" and "Losing Solomon" was reprinted in *Beyond Forgetting: Poetry and Prose about Alzheimer's Disease* edited by Holly Hughes (Kent State University Press, 2008). Reproduced by permission.

"Sundowning" won the Robinson Jeffers Tor House Prize for Poetry selected by finalist judge Robert Pinsky.

"September, North Fullerton Avenue" (under the title "Memory") won the Alsop Review Poetry Competition.

In the poem *Working and Singing*, the lyric from "Wake Up Little Susie" was written by Boudleaux and Felice Bryant. Copyright ©1957 by House of Bryant Publications / Sony / ATV Music Publishing. Renewed 1985. All rights reserved. Used by permission.

The epigraph for section 3 was written by Yosano Tekkan and is reprinted from *Modern Japanese Tanka*, edited and translated by Makoto Ueda. Copyright © 1996 Columbia University Press. Reprinted with permission of the publisher.

I would like to thank Margo Stever, Ann Lauinger, and the Huson Valley Writers' Center, who published my chapbook, *A House That Falls*, winner of the Slapering Hol Press Chapbook Prize, in which several of these poems appear.

I am grateful to the National Endowment for the Arts for their support in the form of a Literature Fellowship in Poetry; the good people at the Arizona Commission on the Arts for their support in the form of a Creative Writing Fellowship and an Artist Project Grant; the ASU Faculty Emeriti Association for the PFF Fellowship; and the Eastern Frontier Education Foundation (Norton Island Residency Program) and the Vermont Studio Center for providing residency fellowships and space. The generosity of these organizations allowed time to write many of these poems.

In the writing of *Oblivio Gate*, I consulted a number of sources for inspiration, and from which phrases and ideas were occasionally referenced. For information about the brain and Alzheimer's disease, I relied on *The Forgetting, Alzheimer's: Portrait of an Epidemic* by David Shenk, *In Search of Memory* by Eric R. Kandell, and *Losing My Mind* by Thomas DeBaggio.

Deepest gratitude to Norman Dubie, Beckian Fritz Goldberg, and Alberto Rios, for their wisdom, support, and friendship during the making of this book and beyond. A sincere thank you to Jon Tribble, Lynne McMahon, SIU Press and *Crab Orchard Review* for helping this book into the world.

I am also indebted to the following friends and mentors for their advice, support, and encouragement: Karla Elling, Gary Short, Wesley McNair, Kimiko Hahn, Liam Callanan, Todd Fredson, Sarah Vap, Nancy Weber, Marianne Botos, George Held, Miguel Murphy, Cynthia Hogue, Jorn Ake, Rigoberto Gonzalez, Kevin Vaughnbrubaker, Peggy Shumaker, Chad Unrein, Casey Charles, Ron Smith, Josh Rathkamp, the ASU diaspora, my friends, my students, and the village. Thanks also to the Young Writers Program and the Office of Youth Preparation,

And finally, a special thank you to Jennifer, who believed me every time I finished this book.

ONE   Losing Solomon

In a dark time the eye begins to see.

—*Theodore Roethke*

Losing Solomon

We estimate a man by how much he remembers.
—*Ralph Waldo Emerson*

Things seem to take on a sudden shimmer
before vanishing: the polished black loafers
he wore yesterday, the reason for climbing
the stairs, even the names of his own children

are swallowed like spent stars against the dark
vault of memory. Today the toaster gives up
its silver purpose in his hands, becomes a radio,
an old Philco blaring a ball game from the '40s
with Jackie Robinson squaring up to the plate.

For now, it's simple; he thinks he is young again,
maybe nineteen, alone in a kitchen. He is staring
through his own reflection in the luster and hoping
against hope that Robinson will clear the bases
with a ball knocked so far over the stadium wall
it becomes a pigeon winging up into the brilliance.

And perhaps, in one last act of alchemy,
as Jackie sails around third, he will transform
everything, even the strange and forgotten face
glaring back from the chrome, into something
familiar, something Solomon could know as his own.

Hippocampus

I like the thought of it, a small sea horse
   curled in the dark coral reef of my brain.
      Hippo from the Greek for *horse*

and *kampos* for *sea monster*. Imagine it
   no bigger than a fingertip, my own
      mounted sentry, stationed there

as gatekeeper to the catacombs
   of memory itself. It's deep
      and alone in the explicit night-sea

of remembering where
   I left my glasses, or in what
      numbered spot I parked the car,

or even in the name of the guy who I was
   certain was supposed to come by sometime
      today to talk about the thing I can't

remember anymore. Nobody's perfect. Oh,
   but when she's humming, my hippocampus
      is beautiful as a wife at a cocktail party

mouthing, like a parrot fish spitting sand,
   the words: *Phyllis—Phyllis—Phyllis*
      at the precise moment

I blankly accept Phyllis-
   from-payroll's clammy hand
      into mine. How lucky

to have this coronated monster,
    this sea horse of memory tucked
        so compactly away in the temporal lobe.

I can almost see it, its spiraling tail
    tethered to the black helix of kelp
        rising from the unconscious,

its long nose and dorsal fin swaying
    against the muted sputter and pull of whitecaps
        listing toward shore. Oblivious

even to the stars streaking through
    the Milky Way, until I call on it again,
        to locate the point of a story that's gone

on too long, and soon a brilliant
    constellation of jellyfish begins to pulse,
        and a trillion bioluminescent algae cells

ignite, like neurons, an entire ocean around it.

Thirty-Nine Years on the Job

For my father at his retirement dinner

If you are tired, you should be—you've worked hard
each day, the schlep into the city, the Johnson File
dog-eared and heavy in your monogrammed attaché.

If you are tired, but still not ready to be retired—get over it,
you are. And although you are not near the fragile figure
that haunts you now, that image of your own father, regretful
and old at his retirement podium some three decades away
forever hunched and expressing into the microphone

his catarrh, you understand that gray can never be the new
black, nor is sixty-five, as promised on the cover of *AARP*,
the new forty, and if history has taught us anything
Dad, it's get out while you still can. So I say this to you

in the spirit of beginnings, and in celebration of the last time
you will be made to dress and answer the tasteless question:
chicken or beef? Now, it's newspapers for you in the long
afternoon light of Korean restaurants, your kimchi chigae
simmering in its stone bowl, and a bottle of beer so cold
the silver crane, as if startled awake, lifts from its fog
and rises through the cloud of frost melting down the label.

Solomon's Tool Shed

The three pine steps
have worn soft.
The sagging runners

bleached from sun
and rock salt,
warped and grain

tattered from boot
treads and spade tips
lifted then dropped

like walking sticks
at the tired end of a day.
The toll of winter's

hammer and grind
grows heavier
each year. Sunlight

worms through
cracked cedar shakes,
vermiculates the dark

clutter of workbench
and plywood wall,
where years of rusted

tools hang on nails
bent like bluefish
hooks. A coping saw

and its dust shadow.
The kitchen clock
whose hands, dizzied

and tired, have given up
the chase. And the one
crimped wood shaving

held in the block plane's
dull blade, furls
like a dried petal,

a forget-me-not.
A small tribute to the end
of beginning new projects.

A settling in, a settling in.

Montclair Vespers

The evening light of suburban New Jersey
has in it smears of newsprint and the khaki
shades of trench coats slung over seatbacks.

Commuters descend, single file,
the concrete stairs at Watchung Station,
each hauling the glum luggage
of shadow hunkered at their clicking feet.

A train's whistle blares behind them,
scatters a murmuration of starling
that swoops down, banks, then doubles back
into itself like a black shawl raised off
the shoulder, alive by wind. It's November

and the maples, having emptied their branches,
rake over their darkening plots of sky.

Walking Bees

My brain skitters from place to place,
unable to alight on a single site
that will provide me with succor or balance.
—Thomas DeBaggio

A mason jar and an arm's length of thread
    sent us out to the thick sprawl of honeysuckle
        draped like centennial bunting along the shed.

Fragrant, steady, flecked with light,
    our hands positioned jars beneath bees
        lost in the silk throat of blossom.

We slammed the lids shut and listened
    for that trapped hum, the irritable drone
        of a motorboat skimming the distant lake.

We were boys, and we controlled nothing,
    except perhaps bees, and the dank world
        found in the imprint of an overturned rock.

We placed the bee jars into a freezer
    and watched, like demented anesthesiologists,
        for the catatonic pith, the thin-veined lamina

that separates living from dead.
    We plucked, with tweezers, the front legs
        like terrible, singed lashes,

and cinched our thread to a hind.
    Pollen sacs gilded our fingertips
        as we laid them out in the grass:

half-drowned bathers, limp and waiting
　　　for the divine sorcery of resurrection
　　　　　to kick in. *Hallelujahs!* They stirred,

punch-drunk, they tested their wings, rose up
　　　and flew hard against the leash.
　　　　　There are acts so cruel in childhood

we don't dare imagine how they must
　　　play themselves out in our absence. How,
　　　　　when the bees finally broke free, they dangled

their one good leg above the nest
　　　like doomed airliners circling the runway.
　　　　　How they would zero in then tick off

the parchment walls until their wings
　　　would rend, until they would drop,
　　　　　like spent petals through air, unable

to clutch at the hive's ashen mouth.

Wildfire Triptych

Fire burns: that is the first law.
—William Carlos Williams

1   What the Smoke Brings

For two full days the sirens
realized their high notes
in the quivering saucers
stacked inside cupboards,
and an exodus of field deer
cropped the blooming gladiolus
down to a stubble.

The wind grew jaundiced,
carried with it a sacrament
of wood ash to the tongue's
sour root, left me raw-throated
and quiet in the car's backseat.

It was a sad evening all day
and the deer, like refugees,
plodded the centers of streets.

I spelled with my finger
the words: *wash me* in soot
on the hood of my father's
Coupe DeVille, as I watched
a six-point buck pause,

then spill a small cache of shit
like polished beads, unstrung
and falling through the yellow
air of the Sears parking lot.

2   Roof Dancer

If the winds swung east
my father would climb
the wooden ladder,

a pail of water weeping
from one hand, and wait
for the first stars to fall.

He'd stamp and douse
the cinders where they'd land
all night. This secret dancing

made weather inside our rooms:
thunder through the bones
of the house, a flurry of snow

descending from the rafters.

3   Variations on Sleep

I

To sleep that night was to travel
    a great distance by train,
        to drag from iron wheels

the crushed chassis of a Ford
    a mile down the tracks, that,
        and a clean rooster tail of sparks

to set the cattails blazing.

II

To sleep that night was to sing
    trainsong falsetto: the lucid song
        of metal gouging metal,

to hear the storm windows rattle
    like teeth in the skull, to know
        fire and the dark brother of fire

careening unhinged.

III

To sleep that night was to work
    worm gears and pistons
        swing shift through the night,

to watch flame carve,
    like a greased machine,
        the hillside, to wheeze

and shimmy oiled phone poles,
       to cleave the roofline
              like a dawn sun, stalled

and dilating above a field.

     IV

To sleep that night was to detonate
       floorboards in dream, to stoke
              the locomotive's blast furnace:

fire-belly barreling through
       the interior, the dried creek beds,
              the bleached crackle of scrub grass

sprouting, at once, into flame.

     V

To sleep that night was to arrive
       a refugee in a foreign station,
              to avert one's eyes and vanish

into the unmapped countryside,
the still-smoldering landscape.

Fainting at My Grandfather's Funeral

I lost my fear of dying
when I slammed my hand
in the passenger-side door
of my father's '61
Cadillac Coupe DeVille

as we waited
for a parking attendant
outside M's Funeral Home.

It was religious, the way
pain shook my hand, hard
and electric, straight through
the bone in my shoulder,

like the funeral director
in his cheap suit, assuring me
with a man's grip and a wink
that it was *alright*, that
he was *sorry for my loss*.

But nothing was alright
and I was not a man,
but a fifteen-year-old boy

who listened to his father
sob quietly all night
through the plaster walls.

And the only thing
I could be sure of
was that I was dying
when the heavy door
swung shut,

and what seemed
like a procession
of translucent moths
flew from my ears
and fluttered against
my burning face.

The entire natural world
transformed itself,
became a silver well shaft,

a disarticulation
of synapse and light
like the crown chakra's
white lotus,

whose petals
began to blossom,
then sparked,
then fell away, until

there was nothing
left of the body

but the ecstatic vision
of the moon-faced valet
gliding toward me,

his tattooed arms extending
right out of their sleeves,
like the two budding wings
                    of an angel.

T W O

Oblivio Gate

Every night the ones who died

come to me and show me their wounds.

—D. Nurkse

Oblivio Gate

By night on my bed I sought him whom my soul loveth:
I sought him, but I found him not.
—Song of Solomon 3:1

I

If we are truly the sum
        of our memories,
                tonight you are not

my husband
        but a young soldier in Korea,
                whispering

across a mud trench in snow.
        You warn me
                about the unpredictable

motions of saw grass,
        about tripwires and crickets
                that seem to answer each other

across a field,
        about the wind, how
                it will always bend a reed

the way a catfish curls
        a cane pole.
                You warn me

about the full moon
      hung out
            like a flare

descending
      beneath a night-cloud's
            silver canopy,

about shadows,
      about the way
            one branch moving

without the others
      means trouble—
            it almost always means trouble.

II

Sometimes
    I'll find you
        sitting upright in bed

bereft as a boy
    who has lost himself
        among the fire-eaters

and drunken barkers
    of the Midway.
        Sometimes

I'll find you twitching
    like a hound in sleep,
        and I pray

you are somewhere,
    howling in the furious
        fanglight of a moon.

Once, as I woke,
    you were simply standing
        naked beside the bed:

a shameless body
    that glowed.
        Your eyes were fixed

to a bare corner of room,
    your head cocked,
        tracking the low gnaw

of wood grubs
    fattening
        in the weight-bearing walls.

III

Movement like this
    becomes a strange calligraphy,
        subtle as the familiar

alphabet of branch shadow
    swept from ceiling to wall
        and back to ceiling.

The grayscale
    of a fine ink opening
        beneath a horsehair brush,

the Korean character
    left drying
        on the page.

Its message
    becomes your insomnia,
        your paper madness.

IV

The moon
    is the rice-paper lantern
        left burning in the garden

long after the last house light
    is put down.
        Wind sweeps its circles

across the empty lawn
    and back again.
        All night

I search you
    for signs of recognition—
        Solomon? Solomon?

I float your name
    out into the darkness:
        a word, a flame,

a silver prayer kite rising,
    rice paper,
        balsa,

twine for the rigging,
    remember this.
        Remember.

V

You are startled and swear,
      the goddamn house
          is lousy with bugs!

Weevils,
      termites,
          the carpenter bee,

the fuckers just burrow and breed.
      Yet somehow
          you knew

about the slow
      tangles and plaques,
          about the snarled web

that blossoms
      beneath the crown molding,
          about the Louisiana weevils

gorging the sweet potato's
      orange meat.
          You knew

about the perforated baseboards,
      about the bees
          that bore

like iridescent drill bits
      through porch,
          about the pelt

of black mold
 alive as a wall rat
  between jack studs.

You knew
 about the dry rot
  in the eaves

and about the palsied signature
 of a worm
  etched across the rotted sill.

You could hear
 the steady gnash
  of mandibles

buried in walls
 like grunts in laced boots
  marching through a frozen field,

like the quick
 electric spill
  of a stroke,

like wood dust,
 and the strange sleep
  that sifts down through stars,

steady as snow,
 forgetting every path
  we've ever walked.

VI

You smiled and said,
    there are so many dreams
        it's hard to pick the right ones,

and I knew you were back,
    for now,
        in the infested body

of this house.
    You cupped my face
        and kissed me

there in our bed
    like a husband, like a man
        on his knees

gulping
    after a thaw
        of river water,

the mouth
    unable to swallow anything
        fast enough.

VII

The mind
      will sometimes turn
            on itself,

the way a stomach will
      devour its own walls
            in hunger.

Gradually,
      you become
            an exposed colony

of termites, writhing
      in the split log of sleep,
            and memory

is nothing more
      than a star-pocked darkness
            that sidles up

like a wife with a toothy smile
      who daubs a damp cloth
            at your forehead,

who calls to you
      down half-lit corridors
            and guides you back

to the familiar wicker chair,
      the lampshade,
            the pillow.

The Korean landscape
      you hung above our bed
            is electric with moonlight

and fever, and somewhere
      in the pasture
            just beyond reason, a line

of stout poplars
      drills holes
            through heavy snow:

a battalion of foot soldiers
      assembles in the tree line,
            bellies through nightwheat and frost.

THREE

Solomon's Palimpsest

In my mind

suddenly it appeared

then passed away.

The black barge with neither

a window nor a light.

—Yosano Tekkan,

translated by Makoto Ueda

Solomon's Palimpsest

I

The darkness you sense
in the half-lit garden
becomes two deer, grazing

themselves into existence.
Their eyes are stoked coals.
Their quick heads

are the shape of anvils
and are forged
entirely of hunger and bone.

They lift, then pause
between the plum tomatoes'
yellow blossoms

as if to take measure
of the world that lies
between themselves

and the whimpering hound
left tied to a spike
in the neighbor's yard.

II

A mongrel bitch
    long-haired and thin,
        she recoils at an airplane's shadow

that scurries across the lawn.
    Its crooked darkness
        triggers memories of the day

a boot lifted her high enough
    to see her own black image
        rushing beneath her.

That same night she couldn't stop
    the five blind pups
        from erupting out of herself,

each a full-bodied howl.
    Her silken uterus
        was a torn purse

slung out
    beneath the sagging porch
        like the uncinched drowning sack

you fished from a stream—
    its slick litter
        left glistening on the mossy bank.

III

This is why she is mad,
       why she snaps at the thread of air
           trailing bees, and runs

herself against the anchored end of rope
       until it creaks, until
           the rope itself moans

around her own neck.
       Because she remembers,
           because she can't forget

the way she carries her ribcage
       like the carcass of a turkey
           broken inside her chest.

For a moment the dog almost seems
       to consider her own predicament,
           as she leans into the tether

and traces her rutted circumference
       that much deeper into earth,
           then settles, then breathes.

IV

At the dog's deep exhalation
    the deer stand,
        black-faced and silent

as two spelunkers
    watching a third descend,
        with ropes, into the breathing

crevasse of consciousness.
    They'll wait for dream
        to set its black flukes

firmly into the mind
    before they advance
        any further down the seed line.

V

You are convinced this is the way
    past lives return,
        slowly and in pairs.

Your parents emerge
    from a darkness,
        a slipstream of memory.

They are standing together
    at the oblivio gate
        framed by the ornate

molding of a doorjamb,
    like an old portrait hanging
        from the sheetrock wall.

Your father's fedora is angled.
    He is silent and thin
        as the coat rack.

Your mother's dress is cotton
    and burgeons with light.
        She steps through shadow,

steals the face
    of the night nurse
        and counts in a whisper

after the trapped flutter of pulse
    alive in your wrist.
        Humming,

she quiets the house lights and waits
    for sleep to rename the bedroom
        hydrangea, 1942.

VI

Dementia is the moonlight scalloped—
    the stunned flit of the yellow jacket
        sealed in a double-hung window,

each thought a stutter against glass,
    a confusion of *world* and *wing,*
        coat rack and *father.*

A bee in the mouth
    of the garden hose,
        the stung tongue

of language,
    the anther, the pistil, the swarm.
        The word salad of object and name

that buzzes the ear.
    The hirsute thorax,
        the venom, the stinger.

The wild flank
    of body vibrating, swelling the brood.
        The blue mud dauber, the carpenter,

the red-tailed bumble, the mason,
    the faithful leafcutting,
        the tarantula hawk, the digger, the honey.

Dementia is the bent monologue
    of shadow flowers, blue-leafed
        and blossoming along the walls.

Through the bedroom window
    you watch the silver
        line of street lamps glow

and shiver like electric hives
  vanishing from their branches
    into fog. One after another

they return: a dim row
  of stammering moons
    that fire on against the night.

VII

You backtalk the dead
  burrowed in the fire pit's
    banked-down embers.

Red-faced and winking,
  they rustle and clack
    false teeth; they chatter and spit

through beards of ash
  until the coals shift, break
    open quiet as a language

starved of fuel.
    And every night you search
      the changing hillsides

in the oil painting
  hanging above our bed—
    the copper hogbacks lifting,

the gulches and peaks;
  the thousand burning leaves
    of autumn

all assume the color of smoldering
  heartwood, cinder and ash.
    The thick brushstrokes

become blue-gray grubs,
  then tragic lips
    pursed and throbbing

into this world
  from another.
    One image gives way

to the next, reveals
>a ghost-text or the lost
>>portrait's yellowed eyes

that seem to shift
>beneath the surface of everything,
>>that skulk through bramble,

that watch the made shoulders
>of moonlight and furniture
>>levitate across the room.

FOUR

Wisdom

And yet perhaps this is the reason you cry,

this is the nightmare you wake screaming from: being forever

in the pre-trembling of a house that falls.

—Galway Kinnell

Wisdom

I've learned, has nothing
in common with the relentless
metronome of carpenter bees
ticking off the aluminum siding

like a steady hail of olive pits
spit through my open window
the summer I learned to shake
martinis without bruising the gin.

Nor does it exist in the imperfect
practice of swatting a strung racket
through the yard after the buzzing
shuttlecock bodies of bees.

This much I've pieced together
from experience, which should not be
mistaken for wisdom.

Wisdom is more
akin to the transformational,

that telephone pole of clarity
arriving from nowhere at 3 A.M.
like a telephone pole,

a kind of cosmic boom
lowered onto the head
of a drunken nineteen-year-old
behind the wheel of his father's
cherry Cadillac Coupe DeVille.

Or in the curiously familiar
stench of my own eyebrows
on fire again,

as I lowered
the fresh Pall Mall
still pinched
in my puckering lips

into the blazing
patch of open flame
between the teriyaki salmon
and the marbled flank steak
the boss was busy grilling
at the company picnic.

Shit happens.

People get fired
and rehired all the time,
but these, these
are the doozies in life,

the *real* hallmarks
from which we grow
a little scar
or develop a tic

we carry quietly with us
for the rest of our lives
as a sort of charm,
a crooked little loadstone,
a scar-tissue medallion

worn on the bridge of the nose
or beneath the twitching eye,
whose sole purpose in our world
is to catch us off guard,

to grab us
as we stride past ourselves
in the mirrored window
of a bank,

to remind us
at the most unlikely of times
we are, all of us, lucky
to be alive.

The Gnome and I Catch Dawn

After memory there is now.
—Beckian Fritz Goldberg

I am confused to find myself
at a loss in this damp garden
beside a ceramic gnome, whom
I appear to have known for years.

The two of us just standing there
dumbstruck in the mulch,
watching the sunrise ignite
windowpane. We can't help
but stare, barefoot and silent
as neighbors in flannel pajamas
gathered at a house fire.

What was there yesterday, today
is gone, vanished before our eyes.
So we wait for someone familiar
to call out from the burning,
for Aurora to remind us of our slippers,
of the pink grapefruit lobotomized
and glistening on the breakfast table,

of the rolled newspaper
already sweating its plastic sheath
somewhere in the overgrown lawn.

The Carpenter Bee

Black and polished
with light, it treads the air
beneath the arched soffits
of our house, where

this morning I smeared,
with a clean metal blade,
a dollop of putty
over the bullet-sized hole
it bore into the wood.

I watched, for an hour
that bee, tap-tap-tapping
like the severed tip
of a cane groping
after what was lost, and

like that, I saw again
the frostbitten toe
the medics let thaw,
then amputated as I slept
through a gauze

of morphine. The charred
and inconsolable knuckle
that would, for years, try,
each night in my dreams,
to come home from the war.

Self-Portrait as Tithonus

Sometimes I enter a room not knowing
the way out, sometimes I'm the kept cricket
chirruping endlessly from the God's Eye
of cobwebs beneath your dresser. Sometimes
I dream from my La-Z-Boy an army
of ants dissecting battlefield corpses
like bruised windfall plums and I fit and claw
the way a mortal thing will, scuttling
its own terrible body. I become
the bat shooed from the rafters, the flutter
off walls until the pin-boned neck fractures
against window. Sometimes I'm the grotesque
muscle thumping, the blind and vulgar heart
lunging toward a small music in the dark.

Self-Portrait as Aurora

Lunging toward a small music in the dark,
that rare glint of recognition, your voice
all but extinct. I part the night's curtain
each day, hoist with my chariot, sunrise
through the just-visible light. A varnished
sheen of dew broadcast everywhere. It slicks
the crickets who babble in the still-dark
thatch, each wet bead cloud-gazing and glossy
as eyes stacked in the monger's window,
slicks each cloud, each squat package sailing
out through the heavens like a regatta
of bulbous vessels, slicks each vessel, each
rigged sail's white and ambling hull with the slick
wake of weeping behind such mortal love.

The Incident

In lieu of sleep
I mimic the garden gnome
for hours. Heels deep
as crocus bulbs,
our elbows fastened
to our hips:

two old soldiers
practicing the slow
tai chi of dementia
in the wild pachysandra.

When a company of ants
stormed the hillock
of his calf, breached
his inner thigh
like a vein gone bad,
all varicose and on the move—
nothing . . . sheer stoicism.

I, for one, had to dance
through the hedges
and out into the road,
tour jeté, chassé,

my terry-cloth robe
unsashed and flapping
in what the police report described
as a moment of weakness
cloaked in exceptional grace.

Sundowning

I

    This white.
                That yellow. This blue.
No matter what color pill
                I crush into the applesauce, this blue bowl,
    to feed you and myself, one
                    full night of sleep, one night
without this wandering. That weeping.
                    Without the long rattle of doors.
Without the all-night cricket clatter,
    and your struggle to shed that yellow
                  wallpaper, that stained skin
peeling from walls. To shed, in this darkness, your bed
    and the white, white infestation of these boards.

II

Each evening that same urge to slip
    this lumbering form, to step from its wreckage as from a robe
    dropped to the floor.
Each evening the struggle to ditch the feeble disguise
              of body, this skin, this jerry-built cage
of bones that holds you, like the rescued starling, disconsolate
    and thrashing
              against its cardboard box.

III

Each evening that blue persistence,

                      that voice, telling you

    to keep an appointment,

                to catch the bus, to report to a job

  lost fifteen years ago, to keep your word,

      to collect the debt, to make things square.

Each evening the struggle to take off your coat, to sit,

                  rest, lie back, to be still.

To sleep one night without this broken clock

    that is you, still chiming

              in this still-blue hour of evening,

     telling you, you are late, overdue.

You are expected somewhere important hours ago.

Years. And you rise, rise

            like bad clockwork. Like I have forgotten.

Like I don't understand.

Like I never understand

         the livingroom drapes are engulfed in flame.

Like the whole damn house of mind

    is burning down around you, and the walls

             are all swallowing their doors.

Again, the Gnome and I Catch Dawn

A house is on fire
somewhere in the mind,
someone is trying to escape,
someone is holding the other back—
—Michael Burkard

Daylight opens across the lawn like disease
this morning, like fire traveling the rafters,

and the gnome and I are listening
to the brutal crescendo of woodworms
spit and sizzle with steam. They hiss
the hiss of the still alive, of the molted
blue claw left spattering in the grease pan,
and they set each riddled plank wailing
like a madman on the piccolo.

What if this is how it happens, how we lose
the stories of ourselves? Our porous bones,
like the timbers they are, already collapsing
into themselves. The burning eaves ready
to buckle from the sudden lightness of it all.

What if this is my life, on fire,
the lit fuse of ganglia and synapse
sparking away with the gilded flecks of ash
that flare then vanish in the plume? What if

my life is the neighbor's howling dog
who has snapped its chain and gone begging
from yard to yard to be taken inside?

Alzheimer's

A blizzard, late in the season, arrives
with its sudden cannonading . . .

It sends a lost soldier wandering, alone
toward the center of what he perceives
as a vast clearing in a dense pine grove.

Snowdrifts will billow up past his thighs,
and the chalk-blue terrain will forget
its own landmarks by nightfall. He will drop

his rifle and his rucksack on the snow,
hallucinate his dead mother
young again, then collapse. Then the moans,

the deep creak and clatter when the gray slab
of lake-ice gives way. A braid of bottom grasses
will hold him down, a frost will heal the sky.

Heart of the Tyrant King

The carpenter bees leave their sawdust dunes
heaped on the porch beneath the wood railing
like ancient pyramids returning to sand,
and the damn termites have taken the walls.

Last night I dreamt I was the dead pharaoh,
the tyrant king mummified in his tomb.
A carved history fading from stone tablets
as looters filled satchels with gold. The worms
had already come and gone, picked the skull
clean. My chest was a winter honeycomb,
a bee's papery nest seized by hoarfrost.

While thieves sifted my organ jars for jewels,
I grinned jawbone through the dim gauze. I felt
the hive stir, all the bloodless wings thrumming.

The Other Dream in Which He Is Weightless

When finally Solomon would drop,
heavy as a scuba diver from a boat,

into sleep, the table fan keeping quiet
sentry over his body, he could practice

the shallow breath of leaving,
push off the bed's earthly pitch, spit polish

his goggles and slip beneath the surface
of knowing. The tired weight of himself

left twitching against his wife. The bedroom
blinds breathing in perfect oscillations,

dawn-purple, cool, and slatted as gills.
When finally he could upend himself,

kick away from this world, follow
the jade columns of light down

and down to the half-sunk mandible of reef,
all molar and bone, barnacle and neon,

he could play again, whirl his diminished body
in circles, the way he used to

tease the neighbor's dog into chasing its own tail.

Hinged Double Sonnet for the Luna Moths

Norton Island, Maine

For ten days now, two luna moths remain
silk-winged and lavish as a double broach
pinned beneath the porch light of my cabin.
Two of them, patinaed that sea-glass green
of copper weather vanes nosing the wind,
the sun-lit green of rockweed, the lichen's
green scabbing-over of the bouldered shore,
the plush green peat that carpets the island,
that hushes, sinks, then holds a deep boot print
for days, and the sapling-green of new pines
sprouting through it. The miraculous green
origami of their wings—false eyed, doomed
and sensual as the mermaid's long green fins:
a green siren calling from the moonlight.

A green siren calling from the moonlight,
from the sweet gum leaves and paper birches
that shed, like tiny white decrees, scrolled bark.
They emerge from cocoons like greased hinges,
all pheromone and wing, instinct and flutter.
They rise, hardwired, driven through the creaking
pine branches tufted with beard moss and fog.
Two green moths flitting like exotic birds
toward only each other and light, in these
their final few days, they mate half-starved, then
wait inches apart on my cabin wall
to die, to share fully each pure and burning
moment. They are, like desire itself,
born without mouths. What, if not this, is love?

Working and Singing

A lemon clip-on earring knocks
against the fat and perfumed cheek
of the Jamaican orderly
leaning in to change the soiled sheets.

She draws your chest up close,
as she does each morning, firm
against her own, then folds
her arms around your back
to free the tucked-in corners.

Her plastic earring bores
into your visions, becomes another
carpenter bee jawing through
the soft wood of memory.

By chance she is singing the song
that you would croon for me
those mornings I'd have given anything
to slip beneath the blankets
and writhe all day against the sun
like the still-blind pupa
exposed in a dry-rotted plank.

She is working and singing
the song I grew first to love,
then dread, because it meant light,
because it meant the unfinished
dream of you had ended,

and left us in this world of swing
shifts, paper cups and yellow pills
ground like pomice into apple sauce
by Jamaican or Haitian mothers
and daughters who too have left
their families, who care for ours,

who work all day and again at night,
who sing the oldies that cough and drone
through transistor radios in rooms
made only of curtain and absolute white.

She is working now, and singing
our song, and somewhere out of a deep
remembering, you fell in tune
with the chorus, sat up and sang along:

wake-up little Susie, wake-up,

like nothing at all had changed, like you
were a child, torn from his own delirium,
from his just-broken fever, sitting there,
so breathless, so ravenous between us.

Elegy

The human tongue, in disbelief, obsesses
at the tender pit of a tooth,

insists on entering the empty room again
and again until it cankers, until even

the simplest word for loss is raw in the mouth.

September, North Fullerton Avenue

The three tomatoes
I picked for the windowsill
against an early frost
hunch and sag in their own skins.

The sweet clot of seed and flesh
rots from within, and a mobile
of delicate insects begins. Fruit flies
seem to appear from nothing.

I watch one, frenzied
in the vapor of decay, measure
and remeasure neurotic circles
like the swung glow of a twig
stoked in a backyard grill.

A lit wand swirls neon
through night's tabula rasa,
its orange trails lingering
just enough to remember

the cursive of a letter,
or the scrawled-out flare
of a name that resonates
long after the burning
fuselage has passed through.

FIVE   Self-Portraits from the Widow House

Grief comes to eat without a mouth.

—William Matthews

Self-Portraits from the Widow House

1   Self-Portrait as the Scavenger Gull

Here at the quiet limit of the world,
   a white-haired shadow roaming emptied rooms, the house
        where my body is ash,   the earth's core still burning.
I chart the ruins daily, tread worn boards,
            each step, charred, compromised.
The scavenger gull, hollow-boned and turning, squawks its gyre.
      I sort the rubble, a toaster, a key chain, your La-Z-Boy chair,
   its slats sprung and laddering up
          like car-struck ribs: a deer carcass
 disarticulated in the purple nap of crown vetch
           wild along the interstate.
The body's rank conversion to gone.
In the aftermath I never return.   I salvage what I can.
I lose everything.

Hauling light through the morose
                   veil of drapes at dawn,
I imagine Tithonus nailed in his dark box. Its cheap pine planks
    knotted with shiners and areolas, the hybrid corpse
               zippered in the sack of rigor mortis.
I am the reluctant survivor babbling our broken parable.
Unable to resist the scene of the crime,
               I mingle like an arsonist, incognito,
   pace the twisted-yellow garland of police-tape
              strung between saplings.
I'm the trench coat, gray tails flapping.
I'm first light's sad throb: night-fog hunkered in the orchard.
To remember, I finger the wound,
            draw air across the cracked tooth,   wince.
To forget, I take the scenic route everywhere, avert my eyes,
   whistle—

3 Self-Portrait as the Emptied Closet

I fan a stack of Manila folders across our bed, warranties,
   the deed to the house. I remove your suit coats, ties—
the shoebox of letters home. I am the emptied closet, the archeologist
   unearthing my own past. In the widow house everything
     is boxed. Moth balls in lace satchels swing from their hangers
        and I hear your impossible footsteps echo
          across the hardwood.   Recollection
   is a treasure map, the fool's errand,
it's flawed, encoded and incomplete. I write history here on the floor.
I still lose.   I must.

Alone in every room, I kiss the plump cheeks of strangers
pawning casseroles in CorningWare dishes.
They wear crocheted oven mitts and stare
through walls. I am blind with grief: a heart
molten beneath a cataract of cheeses.
In the widow house I see people clearly, see,
through two milky eyes, history and tea cups
tremble in the hand, the pages of a book
turn to ash. I gather baubles in the hammock of my blouse,
they are precious, destroyed.
I'll keep them forever.
Processions of cars crowd the street.
At the widow house the streets are barren. I am the last person living.
I learn how little I need.
I need everything, always. Everywhere.

5   Self-Portrait as Scarecrow

A heavy recitation of wood smoke cakes like funeral lime in the mouth.
    I breathe shallow breaths, breathe deeply. I forget how to breathe.
My ancestors swoop, like crows, the fields.
                I'm fixed to a cross, waving—waving,
      my overalls stuffed with straw. I carry my house keys for years,
    refuse to set them down.
                   In the widow house door keys grow huge as axes
  and the Berber carpet crackles at the weight of my feet
              like straw. The world covered in straw.
A vision of spring water cascades down stairwells
        and the faces of loved ones disintegrate like ash.
                  They return in sleep,
  on bicycles, wearing moth-eaten hats.
           This is a blessing.   A kind of prayer.

Splayed as a sulfur moth under glass, sunrise
   is pinned to the sky, and the loam has finally reached its thaw.
Today, I am strong again.
            I carry the earth   beneath my nails, watch the spiders
   return to their spun scaffolds. They are the first
                        to rebuild, to stake their claim,
 to hang their laundry out to dry.   Snails
   decorate the brickwork with their slow tinseled tracks.
Airplanes keen
   like thunderous toys overhead, their contrails dissecting the sky.
And everywhere termites scrimshaw the dead
                    branches beneath sleeves of bark.
Weeds sprout the cracked pavement, the magnolia tree flowers
   from only one side, one side is stripped black with fire.
            I understand this as a kind of mourning.

My heart grown heavy, I become a bronzed statue in a park.   Pigeons
    preen themselves on my head. A thousand feathers zipped and
        unzipped,
  flutter from my rusted cap. I am martyred,   mourned.   Shit upon.
I wear a white tear on my cheek, mourn for what I have lost,
    for what I never had. I become a walking monument. A tribute to loss.
A world champion. I begin to sing
                        folk songs about myself, take a vow of silence.
In the widow house I stay up through the night
    talking and weeping. This is a kind of mourning.
A prayer. I write a book, a song,   the Song of Songs.
        It is riddled with lies.   It's my true story. I burn the book.
Ashes rise through air: a flurry of black snow returning.
This is a kind of mourning.   I never write again.
My life becomes the poem.
                    It is fragmented.   Beautiful.   Flawed.

I lift bowls of tomato soup to my lips, drink loudly, crumble
   saltines through the dark. I'm warmed. I burn
                my morning eggs like two ruined eyes, leave
  the bathwater running for days.
              I cry with the walls, lose
  my keys, my glasses. I step from the shower,
              a lather of soap still in the pit of an arm.
I stand outside in the cold, bicker with the silence then welcome it.
             I lie awake in the cricket chatter, listen
like a lonely dog to the cars turn into the gravel drive,
   watch headlights climb the walls like time-lapsed days.
There are no cars.   I sleep through the night.
                This is a kind of mourning.

I have taken to sleeping in the centers of beds,
I wear, on my wrist, a dab of kerosene and swoon
                              at the pulse in my ear.
It becomes a flint, an anthem, a funeral parade,
                    a message pounded between hilltops,
    a folk song, prayer. It keeps its time. This is a kind of mourning.
In the widow house I live in exile. I'm banished from the past,
    the present. I'm smuggled back in a wagonload of straw.
I'm honored, welcomed with a parade,
                    an oompah-pah band, beer and dancing.
I'm remembered, overlooked, betrayed.   I'm home free, sunk,
    cherished, sung about, persecuted, loved.
                    This is a kind of praise and still, I remain
flammable, highly combustible in public places
                    and all alone. I'm disaster—
the billion sleeper cells ticking, I'm TNT walking.
                    Volatile—this widowheart wired to blow.

Notes

"Losing Solomon" is dedicated to Stephen "Snuffy" Kopec.

The title "Oblivio Gate" uses the Latin *oblivio*, loosely translated as a profound confusion; the term was used in the early study of dementia.

"Walking Bees" is dedicated to Chris Losquadro.

"Solomon's Palimpsest" is dedicated to Dick Nevin.

"Wisdom" is dedicated to my father.

"The Gnome and I Catch Dawn," "The Incident," and "Again, the Gnome and I Catch Dawn" are dedicated to my mother and her gnomes of Wallington, New Jersey.

"Working and Singing" is dedicated to the caregivers.

"Self-Portraits from the Widow House" begins with a line from Alfred Lord Tennyson's poem "Tithonus." The poem is dedicated to Sophie Kopec.

Other Books in the Crab Orchard Series in Poetry